This Mother–Daughter Journal Belongs to:

_____

and

_____

If lost, please contact:

_____

"A mother is your first friend, your best friend, your forever friend."

Date We Began This Journal:

_____

© Copyright,
http://www.CaptivatingJournals.com All rights reserved.
No part of this book may be reproduced in any written,
electronic, recording, or photocopying form without written
permission of the author.

What You can Expect in This Journal/How to Use:

This fun journal has been created for a mother and her adult daughter.

Inside this journal, you will find:

(1.) 2 fun Quizzes, one for mom and one for daughter to learn how much they know about one another.

(2.) 2 Fill-in-the-Blanks Questionnaires — one for mom, one for daughter — No peeking at one another's answers until you both have completed them!

(3.) Mother-Daughter Shared Bucket List to list the things you mutually agree to do together, along with a timeline to achieve these goals.

(4.) Spaces for memorable photos of mother and daughter

(5.) The journal is divided into 2 sections — one for Mother's Questions to answer, and one for Daughter's Questions to answer. You are provided with plenty of space to journal your answers.

(6.) Blank pages so that you can create and customize your own questions to learn about one another. Sample questions have been provided (on the next page) that you can choose what fits your life situations best.

You get to decide how you want to complete this journal, and how you choose to do so may depend on the proximity of mother and daughter (for example, if you don't live in the same city). In this case, the mother may want to complete her pertinent section first, and then send the journal to her daughter to complete her respective journal section. However, if you live close to one another, you may want to take turns completing questions and passing the journal back and forth. There is also no need to journal in any particular order. Take your time and enjoy the journey of learning more about one another, and increasing the bond that only a mother and daughter can share.

"A daughter is just a little girl who grows up to be your best friend."

Other Ideas of Questions to Ask One Another:

Because no two mother-daughter relationships are exactly the same, we have provided you with blank pages at the end of each mother and daughter journal section, where you can add your own questions. Use the list below to generate ideas of questions you want to ask one another..

(1.) What has been the worst day(s) of your life, and how did you move forward and overcome adversity?

(2.) What is the worst trouble that you have ever gotten yourself into?

(3.) What piece of advice would you give your younger self?

(4.) Was there something that your parents did or said that you always said you would never do or say when you were a parent?

(5.) Are there any role models that you admire? Name them, and tell me why.

(6.)   What have been your worst struggles or insecurities (health, emotional, etc)?

(7.) What careers did you consider exploring and why?

(8.) How do you know when it's time to have children? Is there ever a better time?

(9.) In what ways am I like you? In what ways am I unlike you?

(10.) Is there anything you could have done differently as a mother/daughter?

(11.) What frustrated you most about me at times?

(12.) What do you need most from me at this time in our lives?

(13.) When have you been extremely scared in your life? Please elaborate.

(14.) What is your favorite mother-daughter memory?

First my mother, forever my friend.

Photo(s) of Mother and Daughter Together

"A daughter is someone you laugh with, dream with, and love with all your heart."

Mother-Daughter Bucket List

What We Plan to Do Together	Date We Plan to Achieve This By	Date We Crossed it Off Our List

Mother's Journal

This Section is to Be Completed By Mother, & then Shared With Her Daughter

Mother's Memorable Photo(s)

(Insert a photo or two of a memory that means a lot to you)

"A daughter is just a little girl who grows up to be your best friend." – Unknown

Quiz for Mother

How much do you know about your daughter?

HOW TO USE: MOTHER COMPLETES ANSWERS FIRST, & THEN DAUGHTER FOLLOWS SUIT.

The Question	Mother's Answer	Daughter's Answer
What is daughter's favorite TV show?		
What is daughter's favorite food?		
What is daughter's favorite season?		
What is daughter's favorite color?		
What is daughter's favorite movie?		
What is daughter's favorite kind of pet?		
What is daughter's favorite song?		
Who/what is daughter's favorite band?		
Who does daughter most admire?		
What is daughter's biggest pet peeve?		
Where is daughter's dream vacation?		
What was daughter's favorite toy as a child?		
What is daughter's favorite saying?		
What is daughter's past favorite holiday?		
Who was daughter's first best friend?		
Would daughter choose hot or cold cereal?		
Insert your own question here.		
Insert your own question here		

Fill-in-the-Blanks Quiz for Mother

I love my daughter because she is _____.

My daughter loves me because I _____.

I love it when my daughter _____.

My daughter is really good at _____.

My daughter is really smart, because she _____.

My daughter makes me laugh when she _____.

My daughter likes to _____ .

The coolest thing my daughter can do is _____.

I would like to _____ with my daughter.

I would like to teach my daughter how to _____ .

I would like my daughter to teach me how to _____.

One thing I'd like to apologize to my daughter for _____.

One favorite memory spent with my daughter is _____ .

You are never too old to _____.

The day you were born, _____.

My daughter's best attribute is _____.

I would like to travel to _____ with my daughter.

What are your favorite childhood memories?

_____

_____

_____

_____

_____

_____

_____

_____

_____

_____

_____

_____

_____

_____

_____

_____

_____

_____

_____

What were the best things about being a kid when you were growing up? What were the worst things about being a kid then?

_____
_____
_____
_____
_____
_____
_____
_____
_____
_____
_____
_____
_____
_____
_____
_____
_____
_____
_____
_____

How would you describe your relationship with your parents/caregivers growing up, and why?

What are your favorite parts about being a mother?

_____

_____

_____

_____

_____

_____

_____

_____

_____

_____

_____

_____

_____

_____

_____

_____

_____

_____

What are the hardest parts about being a mother?

_____

_____

_____

_____

_____

_____

_____

_____

_____

_____

_____

_____

_____

_____

_____

_____

_____

_____

_____

_____

What was the first year of motherhood like for you? Please elaborate.

Name 3 things that make you most happy. What 3 things make you most sad? What 3 things make you most angry?

_____

_____

_____

_____

_____

_____

_____

_____

_____

_____

_____

_____

_____

_____

_____

_____

_____

_____

_____

_____

What are things you would change about the present and/or the past, if you could?

_____

_____

_____

_____

_____

_____

_____

_____

_____

_____

_____

_____

_____

_____

_____

_____

_____

_____

_____

What do you wish you knew then that you know now, & what would you do differently?

What is the most embarrassing thing(s) that has/have ever happened to you?

_____

_____

_____

_____

_____

_____

_____

_____

_____

_____

_____

_____

_____

_____

_____

_____

_____

_____

_____

_____

_____

What is your best piece of advice for your daughter and why?

_____

_____

_____

_____

_____

_____

_____

_____

_____

_____

_____

_____

_____

_____

_____

_____

_____

_____

Is there anything you would like to share with your daughter, now that she's an adult?

_____

_____

_____

_____

_____

_____

_____

_____

_____

_____

_____

_____

_____

_____

_____

_____

_____

_____

_____

_____

_____

How do you think you know when you find the right person that you want to spend the rest of your life with?

_____

_____

_____

_____

_____

_____

_____

_____

_____

_____

_____

_____

_____

_____

_____

_____

_____

_____

_____

Did you have a best friend when you were growing up, and what did you do together?

_____

_____

_____

_____

_____

_____

_____

_____

_____

_____

_____

_____

_____

_____

_____

_____

_____

_____

_____

_____

_____

What are you most grateful for in this life?

_____

_____

_____

_____

_____

_____

_____

_____

_____

_____

_____

_____

_____

_____

_____

_____

_____

_____

_____

What are your 3-5 proudest achievements in life? Do you have other goals & achievements that you still want to achieve?

What do you think has shaped you into the person you are today?

_____

_____

_____

_____

_____

_____

_____

_____

_____

_____

_____

_____

_____

_____

_____

_____

_____

_____

_____

Do your feelings ever get hurt, and how?

Name 3 things that you're really good at, and 3 things that your daughter is really good at.

I know that my daughter loves me because...

The top 5 things that I would like to do with my daughter this year:

_____

_____

_____

_____

_____

_____

_____

_____

_____

_____

_____

_____

_____

_____

_____

_____

_____

_____

_____

_____

_____

_____

What do you like most about yourself and why? Is there anything that you would like to change and why?

_____

_____

_____

_____

_____

_____

_____

_____

_____

_____

_____

_____

_____

_____

_____

_____

_____

_____

_____

_____

What do I love most about my daughter?

Daughter's Journal

This Section is to Be Completed By Daughter, & then Shared With Her Mother

Daughter's Memorable Photo(s)

(Insert a photo or two of a memory that means a lot to you)

"For all the things my hands have held, the best by far is you." – Unknown

Quiz for Daughter

How much do you know about your mother?

HOW TO USE: DAUGHTER COMPLETES ANSWERS FIRST, & THEN MOTHER FOLLOWS SUIT.

The Question	Daughter's Answer	Mother's Answer
What is mom's favorite TV show?		
What is mom's favorite food?		
What is mom's favorite season?		
What is mom's full date of birth?		
What is mom's favorite movie?		
What is mom's favorite type of pet?		
What is mom's middle name(s)?		
Who/what is mom's favorite band?		
Who does mom most admire?		
What is mom's biggest pet peeve?		
Where is mom's dream vacation?		
What is mom's favorite color?		
Mom's preference – scary or sappy movie?		
What is mom's favorite song?		
What scares mom the most?		
What is mom's favorite saying?		
What is mom's favorite past vacation?		
Insert your own question here		

Fill-in-the-Blanks Quiz for Daughter

I love my mother because she is _____.

My mother loves me because I _____.

I love it when my mother _____.

My mother is really good at _____.

My mother is really smart, because she _____.

My mother makes me laugh when she _____.

My mother likes to _____ .

The coolest thing my mother can do is _____.

I would like to _____ with my mother.

I would like to teach my mother how to _____ .

I would like my mother to teach me how to _____.

One thing I'd like to apologize to my mother for is _____.

One favorite memory spent with my mother is _____ .

You are never too old to _____.

A funny memory of my mother is when she _____.

My mother's best attribute is _____.

I would like to travel to _____ with my mother.

What are your favorite childhood memories?

What were the best things about being a kid? What were the worst things about being a kid?

What do you think shaped you into the person you are today?

_____

_____

_____

_____

_____

_____

_____

_____

_____

_____

_____

_____

_____

_____

_____

_____

_____

_____

_____

_____

What are things you would change about the present and/or the past, if you could?

_____
_____
_____
_____
_____
_____
_____
_____
_____
_____
_____
_____
_____
_____
_____
_____
_____
_____
_____

What do you wish you knew then that you know now, & what would you do differently?

_____

_____

_____

_____

_____

_____

_____

_____

_____

_____

_____

_____

_____

_____

_____

_____

_____

_____

_____

_____

_____

What are your biggest fears and/or concerns for the future, and why?

Do your feelings ever get hurt, and how?

What is the most embarrassing thing(s) that has/have ever happened to you?

_____

_____

_____

_____

_____

_____

_____

_____

_____

_____

_____

_____

_____

_____

_____

_____

_____

_____

What are you most grateful for?

Is there anything you would like to share with your mother, now that you're an adult?

_____

_____

_____

_____

_____

_____

_____

_____

_____

_____

_____

_____

_____

_____

_____

_____

_____

_____

_____

_____

What are your 3-5 proudest achievements in life so far? What other goals & achievements do you want to accomplish in the future?

Name 3 things that you are really good at. Name 3 things that your mother is really good at.

I know that my mother loves me because....

The top 5 things that I would like to do with my mother this year:

_____

_____

_____

_____

_____

_____

_____

_____

_____

_____

_____

_____

_____

_____

_____

_____

_____

_____

_____

What 3 things make you most happy? What 3 things make you most sad? What 3 things make you most angry?

What do you like most about yourself and why? Is there anything that you would like to change and why?

_____

_____

_____

_____

_____

_____

_____

_____

_____

_____

_____

_____

_____

_____

_____

_____

_____

_____

_____

_____

_____

_____

What do I love most about my mother?

"In my life, you are the sun that never fades and the moon that never wanes." — Unknown

Made in the USA
Las Vegas, NV
23 December 2024

15318990R00039